CRUEL AND UNUSUAL PUNNISHMENTS

A collection of plays on words
in verse and prose

CRUEL AND UNUSUAL PUN^NISHMENTS

A collection of plays on words in verse and prose

Perpetrated by
MARK P HENDERSON

Illustrated by
DAVID MOSS

First Published in 2016 by Fantastic Books Publishing
Cover design by Gabi
ISBN (ebook): 9781-909163-14-0
ISBN (paperback): 9781-909163-15-7

Contents

FABLES WITHOUT MORALS

When one of these verses is recited in public the audience expects a carry-home message, and the expectation is always disappointed. The groans are gratifying, though in the interests of health and safety I've sometimes positioned myself within easy reach of the exit before performing a Fable Without Moral. You'll see why.

Most of the following pages are easily understandable by any native English speaker ('Armed with a dictionary,' mutters the Jiminy Cricket voice in my ear), but some specifically British usages could elude natives of our former American Colonies. For example, regular British radio programmes are often preceded, introduced and heralded by an instantly-recognisable piece of music called a *signature tune* – I'm told the American equivalent is 'theme tune'. And a traditional form of British confectionary (a.k.a. 'candy') that remains popular is *Liquorice Allsorts*. These trivial facts are relevant, respectively, to 'The Fox and the Swans' and 'The Death of Icarus'.

Readers who choose to recite any of these pieces to friends or family do so at their own risk.

Mark

The Fox and the Swans

There was an old dog-fox whose teeth had dropped out;
his eyes had grown dim and he suffered from gout.
He lay in his lair, a vulpiform wreck,
and mulled over methods for saving his neck.
'If I'm not to lie here admitting defeat,
I've got to find someone who's easy to eat.'

On a river close by, two swans, newly wed,
kept a family of five on a safe reedy bed.
The dog-fox got wind of them, limped to their side
while their parents gleamed out on the fish-teeming tide
and whispered, 'Come, nestlings, quick, follow me,
and I'll show you such wonders as swans seldom see.'

The five little swans, who of course knew no better,
obeyed the old dog-fox to every last letter,
and once he'd enticed them beyond his front door
he seized them and gobbled them, one-two-three-four;
but the youngest, who'd lagged far behind, being slow,
saw what chanced and ran back to the river below.

It squeaked out the tale of its siblings' sad loss
and the news made its parents exceedingly cross.
To preclude the recurrence of such an event
they dismembered the dog-fox, which made him lament.
The noise that he made as his entrails were strewn
was less of a swan-song than a cygnet chewer chewn.

The Emperor and the Mouse

There was a Chinese emperor
In glorious days of Han –
A handsome, brave and warlike chap,
A perfect sort of man.

His palaces were elegant
And full of silk and gold;
A thousand servants serviced them
And did as they were told –

They polished porcelain vases
And prepared each sumptuous meal,
For if they failed in duty then
The emperor made them squeal.

One day as he traversed his hall
With dignity unhurried,
A movement caught his eye – and there
A little rodent scurried.

Enraged, he raised his sword and spear
And drew his wicked knife
And set off to pursue the mouse
And end its furry life.

The mouse in panic fled; as swift
The emperor gave chase –
Out-scurried by a mouse would be
A terrible disgrace.

He chased the mouse from hall to hall
Through courtyards and through rooms,
Brandishing blades and bellowing
A hundred dreadful dooms.

The servants watched in awe as past
Them all the emperor dashed,
And furniture was overturned
And porcelain vases smashed,

And priceless silks were shredded,
And jewels flung far and wide,
And still the emperor and the mouse
Played on at seek and hide.

The empress sighed and shook her head
And gently tore her hair
As sounds of mass destruction rent
The tranquil palace air.

'Exactly as my mother said,'
Observed the emperor's spouse:
'Chaos reigns whenever there's
A Han about the mouse.'

The Horse and the Wren

A horse, of talent highly rated
and artistic taste refined,
seeking standards elevated,
buildings exquisite designed.
Pencil in his hoof, industrious
at his drawing-board all day,
he drew houses most illustrious,
snacking now and then on hay.

'Twas from fifteenth century Florence
that his inspiration came.
Sketches he poured out in torrents
might have borne Alberti's name:
vaults harmonious, frozen motion,
bright arcades of highest worth,
arches round of sweet proportion
running races in their mirth –

like the Pazzi Chapel, or the
great Medici Library,
or the cloisters of San Croce,
even Orsanmichele.
Idolising Brunellesci,
labouring from day to day,
yet this equine *umanisto*
gave his all for zero pay.

He considered it pathetic
that the modern building trade
by his classical aesthetic
taste was not remotely swayed.
Said the builders, 'Listen, fella,
building things like these, by such
a latter-day Piero della
Francesca, would cost too much.'

Philistines are silly, but'll
always make an artist sick.
He resolved upon rebuttal,
couched in finest rhetoric.
Filled with more than medium dudgeon
by the builders' utterance vile,
still his sentiments curmudgeon-
ly and rude he wrote with style.

What a diatribe he wrote! He's
used sublime hyperbole,
simile, metaphor, litotes,
irony, synecdoche;
ordered, forceful and unpadded.
Said the draftshorse, 'That'll show

them;' and (munching hay) he added,
'Eat your heart out, Cicero.'

Singing joyous near his stable,
a pair of wrens pursued the quest
of gathering all that they were able
so that they could build a nest,
showing not the least remorse as
inter alia they nicked
and lined their new-made home with the horse's
fine sarcastic ungulascript.

The horse was seriously affronted
to find himself by wrens bereft,
but the female thus confronted
him, her feet on spoils of theft:
'Pray consider what you're seeing;
think, dear horse, and don't be vexed;
I've become your Ideal Being:
I'm a wren-ess on sarky text.'

The Cat and the Cash

Beside the hearth, beneath a shelf
that housed a clinking heap of wealth,
a pretty adolescent cat
reposed upon a comfy mat;
but as she dozed, some clumsy clown
contrived to knock the money down.
Coin after coin went falling fast
and landed edgewise, first to last,
upon the hapless feline skull,
split it, entered, filled it full,
until, with metal-coin-stuffed head,
the cat was naturally dead.

Although no doubt this was a pity,
it did put money in the kitty.

Reflections of an Existentialist during his Descent of the North Face of the Eiger

The Eiger's north face soars as sheer as a wall
and it is, I assure you, exceedingly tall.
I'm starting to think that I haven't a hope,
especially since Schumpfinger severed my rope.

Terminal velocity; so fast I descend
that on impact my life-span is certain to end,
but surely I've time to sort everything out
before I touch bottom and flatten my snout.

As Schumpfinger sliced through my rope strand by strand
he explained his decision so I'd understand:
'I deeply regret I must shorten your life,
but you've been consorting with my wedded wife.'

An either-or moment, authentic in act –
no matter if he was mistaken in fact;
I applauded the deed, for by deeds we exist –
no way would I cry, 'Sir, you err! Pray desist!'

Now the wind past my ears makes a whistling noise;
on the ground far below me the pines look like toys;
ironic, I smile as my past is unfolding,
my favourite novel is 'Free Fall' by Golding.

What price posterity, what value in fame?
we end in oblivion, no god to blame;
no one will miss me or mourn me, I trow,
excepting, allegedly, Schumpfinger's *Frau*.

In useless reflection our mind ever delves,
we only in moments of truth find ourselves.
We have seconds, or years, as chance will allow,
but as Tillich once taught, time's eternally Now.

Ideas we inherit are fruits of confusion,
idealists and dualists are steeped in delusion.
The Cosmos is big – it extends everywhere –
but no one would miss it if it wasn't there.

The ground rises rapidly, eager to meet me,
but several firemen are there now to greet me;
a trampoline-like sheet they have stretched overhead
so rather than rocks I strike rubber instead.

Sir Isaac once clearly predicted the sequel:
reaction ensues and it's opposite and equal.
With a twang of the sheet my descent I retrace
and return to my perch on the Eiger's north face.

My climbing companion observes my return
with a start of surprise and a look of concern;
from his handhold I Schumpfinger blameless dislodge
and he plummets to earth with a succulent splodge.

Perhaps now, I muse as I watch him depart,
his widow and I can make a fresh start.
I reflect, while descending the orthodox way,
how the schemes of a Schumpfinger gang aft agley.

The Death of Icarus

When Daedalus and his son were locked away
Securely in a cell above the bay,
The old inventor soon devised a trick
(Incarceration getting on his wick)
For making their escape. He charmed the birds –
They say he always had a way with words –
And robbed them of their feathers, which he bound
Together using wax that he had found
(No, that's enough – we won't discuss the source)
And made two hefty pairs of wings, of course.

'Now we can fly this nest,' quipped Daedalus,
'Leaving our captors here to swear and cuss.
But listen, son, fly straight and not too high;
Remember that the sun is in the sky.
It's hot up there, and if it melts the wax

Your wings will fail, and surely it won't tax
Your intellect to see the consequence:
There won't be time for your resipiscence.'

Of went the pair on artificial wings,
Experiencing the joy that freedom brings,
Borne on the air above the wine-dark sea,
Seeking a place where they could stop for tea.
Old Daedalus flew on, wondering as ever
How 'twas he always proved so very clever,
And failed to notice how his son ignored
His guidance: oh, so very high he soared!

They say he flew too near the sun and so
The wax was melted. 'Twas too long ago
For certainty, so maybe that's a fiction;
Perhaps the wax was liquefied by friction.
In either case, just as anticipated
One artificial wing disintegrated,
Plunging him down to Neptune's wet dominion.
The cause was just a matter of a pinion.

Sea-maids who swam the waves thought it appalling
To see the poor young helpless fellow falling.
Quickly they congregated right below him
And hatched a nifty plan to stop or slow him:
They took a harp from Aeolus, which they held
Above their heads so that it paralleled
The surface of the sea. Their act was spirited;
Their scientific knowledge limited.

So fast was he descending, on arrival
There was a zero chance of his survival.

Aeolian harps were twenty-stringed devices;
He went right through in twenty-one thin slices.
The sea-maids drew a sad collective breath –
They knew the meaning now of 'dice with death';
But though the young man's passing was lamented...
That is how Icarus Allsorts were invented.

Hamish: a Cautionary Fable

On Hamish – (what's his name?) – McTavish
    Sympathy you must not lavish;
    You should not his fate bewail
    In this instructive moral tale.
    He was a master of deception,
    Sly obreption and subreption,
    Always apt to chance his luck
And seek to make a dubious buck.

    He seemed to ply an honest trade
    And for his labours he was paid
    As painter and as decorator –
    Quite an income generator.
    Trade for him was never slow

For Hamish kept his prices low,
So he won contracts far and near;
Success, thought all, in his career.

How did he keep his prices down?
The question spread from town to town;
But never were his means detected,
Nor were they even much suspected.
Hamish, I fear, was not a saint;
Invariably he thinned his paint:
A tin for ten square yards proved plenty,
Made dilute, to cover twenty.

When the preacher launched a search
For one to paint the Baptist church,
His team of trained negotiators
Talked to a dozen decorators.
True to their businesslike agenda
They opted for the lowest tender;
Thus, despite his plan to rob,
Hamish McTavish got the job.

With paint well thinned he set to work
And smirked a surreptitious smirk.
He painted all the roof sky blue,
And made the walls look good as new,
He brightened up the double door,
The window-frames, the steps, and more –
But judgment now was beckoning
And soon there came a reckoning.

The sky grew dark, the clouds grew thick,
And then (it made McTavish sick)
Torrential rain began to fall
And washed the paint from roof and wall.
The storm left Hamish in the lurch;
For very soon the Baptist church
Was just as ere the job was started.
Hamish stood soaked and broken-hearted.

Lightning flashed and thunder cried –
McTavish soon was terrified
And fell upon his knees dismayed
And for forgiveness loudly prayed.
The sky grew darker still, like lead,
And from directly overhead
There came the loud celestial roar:
Repaint! Repaint! And thin no more!

TALES TO TELL

when you want to alienate your family and friends

The following fifteen vignettes constitute a selection from the extensive repertoire available to us.

Out of consideration for our readers we haven't included more.

Joe the Jewel Thief

Joe was accomplished, well-respected and adept at avoiding detection. He'd served two short terms in prison but had never been convicted of a major crime. His usual *modus operandi* was to remove diamonds and other gems from jewellers' shops, working with only one or two accomplices, and to hide the haul in a place from which it would later be recovered by trusted colleagues who had not been involved in the theft itself. A sale would then be arranged and the profits would be shared.

Joe's heists were carefully planned and organised and meticulously executed. However, he had one characteristic that caused covert amusement among his co-workers and also among the police: whenever possible, he expressed himself through traditional proverbs and wise sayings. For example, when his reconnaissance and other preparatory work indicated the need for two accomplices during the theft, but three or more had gathered for the planning meeting, he would observe: 'Too many cooks spoil the broth'. If more accomplices were required and too few had foregathered, he would remark: 'Many hands make light work'. During the robbery he would indicate the need for caution by admonishing his companions to 'Look before you leap', but when haste was required he would tell them 'He who hesitates is lost'. Sometimes a proverb or wise saying would serve as a code, identifying the hiding place he'd selected to those whose task was to recover the stolen goods.

When a leading jeweller's was raided and two small bags of highly-priced diamonds were stolen, Inspector Grabbem of the Yard was convinced Joe was involved. Alas, there was no evidence. The alarms had been inactivated, the CCTV cameras had mysteriously failed, and there were no witnesses. Inspector Grabbem obtained a search warrant for Joe's house but of course nothing incriminating was found. He directed his investigating team to research Joe's movements over the past few months. Nothing suspicious came to light, but the inspector had an intuition. Recently, Joe and his friends had frequented a restaurant and bar called The Hive. Could a clue be found there?

The Hive was an up-market establishment on the edge of town. Many of its habitués were members of the Rotary Club and were often to be seen on the nearby golf course. The management, waiters and regulars of The Hive were interviewed. None had a bad word to say about Joe and his friends. None had any inkling that Joe could have been involved in a jewel theft. But Inspector Grabbem persisted.

At last, a chance remark encouraged him. A fortnight previously, the neon sign above the main door of The Hive had ceased to light. Joe had recommended a team of electricians – friends of his – who would repair the connection free of charge. The management had been delighted, the electricians had been called in, and the neon sign was now working again; or almost working. Six of the seven letters constituting the restaurant's name were consistently illuminated, but the fifth of the seven remained dark. Joe had promised that his friends would return to complete the repair within the next week.

Grabbem now knew what was afoot. He arranged twenty-four hour surveillance of the front of The Hive. Sure enough, a few days later, Joe's alleged electrician friends appeared with step ladder, tool bags and boiler suits. They erected the ladder, climbed up to the sign, removed the fifth letter, made some adjustments and set about replacing it. But through his binoculars, Grabbem had seen the workmen extract something from within the neon tube and secrete it in a tool bag. He gave the order to apprehend the men. The electricians saw the police moving in on them and bolted, but they were soon caught. In the tool bag were the two little bags of diamonds.

Grabbem's colleagues were impressed by this masterpiece of detection. 'How did you find out?' they asked. 'There was hardly a single clue.'

'Ah,' replied the inspector, 'it was a matter of knowing Joe's way of thinking and speaking. He needed to tell his accomplices where the jewels were hidden. Once we knew his recent movements, it didn't take long to work out what he'd said to them: *Booty is in the 'I' of the bee holder.*'

Mendel and the Novice

In 1936, the distinguished statistician R. A. Fisher observed that the data published in Mendel's famous paper about hybrid forms of garden peas – the supposed founding document of genetics – seemed 'too good to be true'. However, Mendel was known to be an honest and careful worker. He wouldn't have dreamed of cheating. Besides, he was a monk.

Recent research has implicated his assistant, Willi the Novice, in ensuring that the results were a near-perfect fit to the theoretical trait ratios.

Willi wasn't dishonest by nature; he was a kind-hearted young chap who didn't want the likeable Gregor Johan to be disappointed. So, following traditional recipes, he obtained vegetable dyes and other extracts from wild flowers that grew in odd corners of the monastery grounds, and devised ways of applying them to selected pea plants so that the leaves and the pods and their contents became bright green, or yellow, or wrinkly, as appropriate. The trick, as he discovered through trial and error, was to apply the vegetable extracts while they were hot. He would spend hours in the kitchens when Mendel wasn't looking, cooking up his brews until they steamed, and then scuttle out to the vegetable garden with a bubbling pan in one hand and a brush in the other and surreptitiously set to work. He went on hand-pollinating the flowers and producing the crosses as Mendel instructed, but as soon as he divined what results the boss was looking for, he used his vegetable concoctions – especially the bubbling pans of dye – to ensure that the 'right' results were obtained.

It was a lot of work, and Willi had to be very careful how he went about it. It wouldn't have done to make the peas wrinkly when they should have been yellow. He had to be meticulous in both the official pollination and seeding work and in his clandestine manipulation of the outcomes. In fact, he became a by-word for pernickety attention to detail: always careful to hot his dyes and cross his peas.

Raiding across the Wall

Hadrian's Wall was built as a physical indicator of the northernmost extent of the Roman Empire, but it served an immediate practical purpose: it was a barrier against the depredations of the less Romanised tribes who dwelt in those regions of Britannia closest to the Arctic. These Caledonian tribesmen had formed the habit of making lightning raids into the civilised parts of the island, later known as Northumbria, nicking whatever they could, and scurrying back home again before the legionaries – typically chilled, homesick, intoxicated, and generally hacked off with life in the far reaches of the Empire – could apprehend them. But the Wall thwarted the northern tribes. No longer was it so easy to nick stuff from the Romans and their local allies.

However, these proto-Scots were a cunning and canny people. There was no way they could climb the Wall, make the raid, climb it again and go home without being caught and suffering unamusing consequences, notwithstanding the low spirits of the legionaries. But if they had a ladder …

After a meeting of tribal elders it was decided that a party of men would take food, wrapped in leaves and pieces of hide, and eat it in the shelter of the Wall. There could be no harm in that from the Roman perspective. But after a few such *al fresco* repasts there was a substantial heap of discarded leaves and hide around the base of the Wall. Then, under cover of darkness, it took only a few seconds for the raiding party to scamper up the heap of debris, leap over the Wall, nick whatever they could carry, and scurry back again.

This tradition survived the Fall of the Roman Empire and persists today, not only around Hadrian's Wall but all over the country. Nowadays, in place of biodegradable wrappings, the *al fresco* diners deposit plastic wrappings and sheets of tinfoil, which persist indefinitely.

However, the old name for the practice has survived; it's still known as Pict nicking.

Reflecting on Poet and Philosopher

A few nights ago I was re-reading the fourth book of Horace's Odes, written in about 15 BCE, and the opening line of the first poem in the collection resonated with me: *Non sum qualis eram bonae sub regno Cynarae.* The English translation is 'I am not as I was under good Cynara's reign', and the poem goes on to request the goddess of love to leave Horace in peace because he's now too old for that sort of thing.

Separate the opening phrase from its context, though. When you're feeling your age, just those first four words of the poem say it all: *Non sum qualis eram.* 'I am not what I was.' It's a mildly depressing reflection.

But – I thought – suppose you were to couple it with the famous phrase attributed to René Descartes: *Cogito ergo sum* ('I think therefore I am'). This would generate a happier and more positive reflection: *Non sum qualis eram, sed cogito ergo sum* ('I am not what I was, but I think therefore I am'). Yes, indeed. Maybe I'm getting older, but my mind still works, so I haven't lost either my identity or my pleasure in life (love is another matter, but let us leave that to the poet).

However, it would be less pleasing if the phrases were coupled the other way round: *Cogito ergo sum, sed non sum qualis eram* – 'I think therefore I am, but I am not what I was'. This would be sad. It seems to say that my mind still operates, but not as well as it used to because I'm deteriorating.

It would be wrong to arrange the phrases in that more negative order. It would be putting Descartes before the Horace.

Amphetamine from Rodents

One of the health hazards of amphetamine use – apart from cardiovascular pathology, increasing nuttiness and slimming – is the tendency of habitual users to chew the insides of their lips and cheeks, sometimes making holes in them. This behavioural freak of speed-heads probably results from the dry mouth caused by the drug, coupled with the sense of excitement and restlessness it induces.

It is a little known fact that certain rodents, notably hamsters, produce significant quantities of phenylmethylketone, a precursor of amphetamine. If a purée of a suitable rodent is cooked at high temperature under dehydrating and anaerobic conditions for a couple of hours, ammonia released from the breakdown of endogenous amines will convert the aforementioned phenylmethylketone to amphetamine.

Therefore, if a speed-head homogenises a number of hamsters and mixes the homogenate with (say) an equal weight of granulated sugar and cooks the whole mess up in a covered pan, and then eats some of the proceeds, he will get *chew-lips from hamster jam.*

Cartoon Treatment for Depression

During the 1950s and early '60s two American psychoanalysts, Levine and Redlich, pioneered a new diagnostic (and potentially therapeutic) technique in the area of psychiatric illness. It depended on abnormalities in the recognition of and response to humorous situations. The two investigators cut cartoons out of the New Yorker and other magazines, and appointed a panel of independent judges to (a) categorise these images as sick, sexual, whimsical etc. and (b) rate them on a scale from 1 to 5 according to humour value. Then they examined responses to them. (They added a set of non-humorous pictures as controls.) The responses of 'normal' subjects corresponded with the ratings agreed by the independent judges, but psychiatric patients showed occasional abnormal responses – either laughing inordinately at unfunny pictures, or failing to see anything amusing in hilarious ones.

This procedure scored successes. One patient, a very able company director, had a serious anxiety neurosis. Neither he nor the doctors had been able to identify the root cause of his anxiety. However, one of the cartoons in the diagnostic kit portrayed an office reception area window beside which was a 'suggestions' box; someone had put a bottle labelled 'poison' on top of the suggestions box. The patient stared at this cartoon and declared he didn't see the joke. So Redlich asked him to describe the picture in detail. The patient obliged, describing the reception area, the window, the suggestion box and the bottle ... the one thing he didn't describe, because he literally couldn't see it, was the label saying 'poison'. Source of anxiety revealed: the poor chap believed that his employees disliked him and wanted to be rid of him, but he was unable to admit it to himself.

The story goes that with progressive refinements of their diagnostic kit, Levine and Redlich achieved the construction of a cartoon so hilarious that no one, irrespective of depression, anxiety, schizophrenia or plain normality, could help but laugh uproariously at it. The therapeutic value of this ultra-cartoon was widely recognised and hailed as a breakthrough in treatment.

In due course, a colleague from a distant state contacted the two innovators and asked for their help with a patient so deeply sunk in depression, so unresponsive, that the case seemed beyond hope. Everything had been tried: drug treatments, ECT, occupational therapy ... So, armed with the ultra-cartoon, Levine and Redlich travelled to the distant state and visited the clinic housing the patient. They decided to leave a copy of the cartoon in the patient's room and wait for him to fixate on it. In the interim, they went into town for a cup of coffee, accompanied by the patient's personal therapist. While they were in the cafe the town's inhabitants were startled by a colossal explosion, which had come from the clinic.

'What happened?' said Levine.

'Just what I feared,' said their colleague. 'A huge bang is to be expected when an irresistible farce meets an immovable abject.'

Chou's Chippie

'What do you mean, order a Chinkee from the chippie?' she asked.

Her bewilderment was understandable. In Scotland, a chip shop is a *chippie* and a Chinese takeaway is a *Chinkee Kerryoot*, and never the twain shall cohabit under one roof. I had to explain that things are different in England: one can purchase fish and chips with vinegar, and sweet and sour prawn with fried rice, over the same counter at the same time. She made a racist comment about English people and especially their chip shops.

'There's nothing but fish and pies. No black pudding or white pudding suppers or haggis suppers or deep fried pizzas (I love a deep fried pizza) or sausage suppers or–'

'But there are Chinese meals, and I suggest we order one. Chou's stuff isn't bad. His beef with green pepper and black bean sauce is excellent.'

'Och, I'll just have a fish supper.'

So I took my place in the six o'clock queue and ordered a portion of fish and chips (brown sauce, not vinegar) and a portion of beef with green pepper and black bean sauce with fried rice. She'd probably try some of it and donate half her chips to me. But poor Chou was under stress. Two of his regular helpers were missing, there was more than a shop-full of other customers, and the phone was yapping its receiver off like a crazed Chihuahua. Chou was working alone: taking orders, cooking meals, serving them, and answering the dog and bone. His harassment was tangible.

The poor fellow was stir-frying my meal (with fried rice) with consummate Oriental skill but failed, amid the plethora of demands on his attention, to supervise the high-quality fish frizzling in the fryer. While Chou stirred the contents of his wok with all the passion of the born chef, the fish acquired the consistency of battered hardboard.

Shaking with mirth, I was obliged to leave the shop. My companion followed me out.

'What's the matter with you?'

'Didn't you see?' I spluttered. 'Chou is the first person I've ever seen who's literally been caught between a wok and a hard plaice.'

The Tale of Perilaus and Phalaris

Recently, I made a brief trip by time machine to 6th century BCE Akragas to visit the tyrant ruler Phalaris. Phalaris had a twisted sense of humour; he amused himself by throwing his political opponents into the crater of Mount Etna. I wanted to meet him to discover the truth behind the legend of Perilaus.

According to the story, Perilaus was a gifted metal-worker who constructed a life-size, hollow bronze image of a bull. This beautiful sculpture was designed to enable Phalaris to practise his favourite entertainment in the comfort of his own palace instead of having to climb all the way up Mount Etna. The person who disagreed with the tyrant was to be placed inside the bronze bull, under which a fire was then lit. The protestations of the bull's roasting occupant would be transmuted (thanks to a delicate set of pipes set in the statue's nostrils) into a melodious mooing.

Notwithstanding his predilection for cruelty, Phalaris considered this invention a step too far. He expressed his critical reservations by having the bull's creator, Perilaus, placed inside it and cooked. He and his friends then enjoyed a banquet, with lots of wine, accompanied by the melodious mooing. It saved having to pay the court musicians.

I had a number of questions for Phalaris. For example, if the events of the tale had really happened, what had become of the bull subsequently? Somewhat to my surprise, I discovered that the legend was largely true, but there was an unrecorded twist in it that explained why the use of the bull was a one-off.

By chance, I arrived in 6th century BCE Akragas just after Phalaris had decided to put Perilaus into the bull and cook him. One aspect of the tyrant's character that quickly became apparent was that, like many warlords before and since, he respected enemies who retained a stiff upper lip while being tortured to death but despised those who cracked or sought to accelerate their demise. Perilaus, realising that his sentence was unlikely to be mitigated, and not having the kind of macho courage that Phalaris liked to see in an enemy (the sort that encourages tough guys to cut their feet off with chainsaws just to prove they can), covertly opted for acceleration. As the legend implies, he was a very skilled craftsperson. *Inter alia*, he had devised explosives. He might have pinched the idea of gunpowder from the Chinese; the silk route was a going concern even then. He therefore secreted a quantity of explosive about his person. I didn't ask where.

Phalaris kindly invited me to share his banquet, wine and entertainment, and, being surrounded by half his army, I accepted. The mooing from the hot bull depressed my appetite, but I made a show of enjoying myself; one must try to be a good guest, especially in 6th century BCE Akragas. Soon, however, there was a tremendous bang from the lower end of the hall and the bull disintegrated in a shower of smoke, sparks and shrapnel. Everyone was startled. Phalaris made an elaborate gesture of contempt and loathing that entailed spitting out his wine and insulting several gods simultaneously and viscerally.

'Excuse me, sir,' I said, 'but don't you think we should go and see what's happened?'

'No,' he replied curtly. 'Not yeti.'

'You mean 'not yet'?' I hazarded.

'No. Yeti. A bomb in a bull's no man.'

Briar Pipes

Beside the lake grew thick briars, and Old Pete fashioned pipes from the wood. Old Pete's pipes were works of craftsmanship; large and small, they were a joy not only to use but to behold. People from far and wide came to Old Pete's cabin beside the lake to purchase his creations. Smokers declared that no better pipes were to be found anywhere in the world, and non-smokers bought them to display in glass cabinets or on mantelpieces. More surprisingly, musicians discovered that they could be played like woodwind instruments, producing a pure but mellow sound that reminded listeners of the songs the birds sang beside the lake where Old Pete lived. For this reason the pipes came to be dubbed 'lake horns', and Pete took to marketing them under that name.

One Christmas, Ben and Chrissie acquired a quantity of cannabis resin and resolved to smoke it. Neither was partial to tobacco, so they decided that a good-quality pipe was needed. Their friend Mickey suggested they buy a couple of pipes from Old Pete. He drove to the cabin beside the lake, taking Ben and Chrissie with him.

'We'd like a couple of lake horns, Pete,' said Mickey.

'All the ones hanging on that wall are for sale,' said Old Pete. 'Take your pick.'

Ben, Chrissie and Mickey studied the collection and at length decided on their purchases. Ben and Chrissie bought a large pipe, Mickey bought a small one, and they set off home. Ben gave Mickey a piece of the hash as a token of thanks for recommending Old Pete's pipes and for acting as chauffeur.

Ben and Chrissie found their pipe disappointing. No doubt it would have been wonderful for tobacco, and it produced a delightful musical sound, but the hash wouldn't burn in it. All efforts to use it proved frustrating. Ben phoned Mickey.

'This pipe doesn't work,' he complained.

'Yeah … well … mine does,' slurred Mickey.

'Any chance you can bring it round here, or should we come to yours?'

'Maybe best come here. I might get lost.'

So Ben and Chrissie drove to Mickey's flat. It took Mickey some time to let them in. Then he handed his small pipe to Ben, who put a piece of hash into the bowl and lit it – and it burned beautifully. Before long, Ben and Chrissie were as high as Mickey.

'Just goes to show, size isn't everything,' observed Chrissie.

The hash was still burning in the bowl of the small pipe, lighting the sweet-smelling grey fumes from below so they became quietly incandescent – a pleasure to observe as well as to inhale.

'Yep,' agreed Mickey, studying the pipe and taking yet another draw of the fumes. 'Grey tokes from little lake horns glow.'

A Conservationist Farmer

Jack's farm lay near the sea. The soil along the coastal strip was thin and acidic, covered in the summer months with heather and wild thyme and bare rock, but the fields further inland were fertile and the soil friable, excellent for cereal crops. Jack grew wheat and barley, using organic farming methods as far as possible, and he also kept stock – dairy cattle, some poultry, a couple of horses, sheep on the higher ground. The manure was either ploughed back into the land or used to generate methane. He'd converted his tractor and his Land Rover to run on methane.

Over the years, Jack had experimented with farm equipment design. Because of the quality of soil in his fields, he'd had some success with ploughs made of deer antlers and the shoulder blades of oxen; they didn't last as long as metal ones but they were cheaper – and when they broke they could be recycled, dried and ground up for bone meal. These ploughs could be drawn behind the methane-driven tractor and, with sufficient patience, used effectively over many acres. Jack was encouraged to construct other equipment from recyclable materials.

After much trial and error, he discovered that equipment for breaking up the soil surface and covering newly-planted seeds could be constructed from the herbs that grew along the coastal strip. Bound together with twine and brambles over a six-foot-square area, the roots of these herbs could break up lumps of earth and reduce them to fine powder, and they proved durable. With great care and some excitement, Jack assembled the equipment and hitched it to the back of his tractor. Then he set off along his biggest field, dragging the contraption behind him and creating a pleasingly smooth and level tilth in his wake.

Unfortunately, when he reached the end of the field and turned to go the other way, the equipment ceased to work. Either it wouldn't go, or it wouldn't do anything. He returned to his starting point and dragged the thing in the same direction as he'd first taken. It then worked well; it just wouldn't go the other way.

Of course, the harrow of thyme only goes in one direction.

Manuel the Clown

The circus was in town and there was great excitement in Mexico City, but what use would the circus be without its best and funniest clown? Manuel had taken a holiday and was living it up as only the best and funniest of clowns can do in the middle of the Mexican desert. The circus master was beside himself.

'Bring Manuel back immediately! The circus can't go on without him!'

'Yes sir,' he replied from a little to his left.

So off went two of the circus master's minions to find Manuel, the best and funniest of clowns. They located him in a part of the desert awash with absurd cacti.

'Quickly, Manuel! You must return to the circus without delay!' cried the minions, trying to bundle the clown on to a fleet-footed stallion.

Alas, a clown's massive feet are hopeless in the stirrups of fleet-footed stallions. The stallion departed, leaving Manuel prone in the desert dust, visible only by his big red nose and checked attire.

'What do we do now?' wondered the minions.

They decided that Manuel might be able to ride a burro. So they borrowed a burro. But it was useless. Manuel managed to sit on the burro, but when the burro moved forwards, Manuel fell off at the tail (the blunt end). He was replaced on the animal's back, but when the burro stopped, he fell off at the nose (the sharp end). If the burro turned right, Manuel fell off to the left. If the burro turned left, Manuel fell off to the right. Progress was nil.

So the minions were obliged to phone the circus master, who was apoplectic. He would have to send a helicopter to collect Manuel, the best and funniest of clowns.

'What did you think you were doing, trying to make him ride a burro?' he screamed.

'Well, we thought it seemed like the best and likeliest …'

'Of course it wasn't! Are you totally ignorant? Don't you know that a mule and his funny are soon parted?'

The Gunslinger

The sun was rolling on its back in the west, scarring the sky with gashes of red and orange. Dust and sand spiralled from the meandering trail among jagged boulders, curdled tufts of grey sagebush, cacti, and the desiccated skeletons of the long-forgotten. Hardly a vulture stirred.

The gunslinger raised the collar of his leather coat and pulled the brim of his hat down over his eyes. His horse, an exhausted Appaloosa, lurched and stumbled into the silent town: ramshackle storefronts, a dilapidated general store, a weathered saloon. The stillness swallowed the sound of the hooves on the dust of the main street.

The gunslinger dismounted in front of the saloon, tied the Appaloosa's reins to a worm-eaten post at the roadside, lifted his rifle from the saddle and strode through the classic swinging doors into the building. A fat perspiring bartender with a limp moustache and a bald pate turned his suspicious face towards the newcomer. Silence fell among the patrons; drinks were quietly lowered to tables. All eyes turned to the gunslinger as he slammed his rifle on to the bar and threw a handful of coins on to the stained wooden surface.

'Gimme a shot of redeye.'

'Sure.'

The bartender gave him a whiskey. The gunslinger seized the glass, flung the firewater down his throat in a single motion, and demanded another.

'Hey, Mister,' observed the bartender, presenting more whiskey, 'there's five notches in the stock of your rifle. What they mean, huh?'

'Five Apaches ambushed me.' The gunslinger savoured his redeye. 'Fed 'em to the coyotes.' He patted his rifle. No one moved, but everyone in the bar seemed to back away from him.

The gunslinger finished his redeye, nodded to the assembly, and left the saloon. The sound of the Appaloosa's hooves faded into the darkening desert. Silence returned to the town.

A few weeks later, the sun westering, the dust silent, the gunslinger returned. Tying the Appaloosa to the same worm-eaten post he strode into the saloon and up to the bar, and demanded a shot of redeye. His beloved rifle lay close to hand on the stained wooden surface.

'Hey, Mister,' observed the barman, handing over the glass, 'there's *ten* notches in the stock of your rifle now. What's that mean, huh?'

'Five outlaws. Bounty on 'em. Been huntin' 'em since they robbed the bank in Reno.' The gunslinger shook the heavy bag of coins fastened to his belt, and swallowed his redeye. 'Guess the vultures had themselves a feast.' He grinned.

Once more, the occupants of the bar seemed to back away from him without moving. The gunslinger finished his redeye, nodded to the assembly, and left the saloon. The sound of the Appaloosa's hooves faded, and silence returned.

A few weeks later, the same scene was repeated: westering sun, dust, silence; and the gunslinger appeared again.

As the bartender handed over the shot of redeye, he saw twenty notches on the stock of the gunslinger's rifle. He asked the question.

'Gang of five Mexican bandits. Didn't stop to bury 'em.'

There was the usual sense of backing away; but the bartender continued, a little tremulously: 'Yeah, sure, Mister, but there was ten notches on your rifle last time you was by. Then you shoot five Mexicans. Don't that mean there should be fifteen notches now? You got *twenty*, not fifteen.'

'Sure,' drawled the gunslinger. 'But it was bonus notches for the Mexicans.'

The Financial Disaster that befell Lord Hittle

Percival, 3rd Viscount Hittle, loved the theatre to the point of obsession. When he succeeded to the title and found himself burdened with an expensive and decaying family home and inheritance tax, he wondered whether his greatest passion might serve to restore his fortunes. He secured the services of a celebrated architect to convert the great banqueting hall of Hittle House into a theatre. Banquets formed no part of Percy's plans for the future, but plays did.

The architect, an honest if laconic fellow, succinctly foretold disaster; but Percival, 3rd Viscount Hittle, would have none of it. Plans were drawn up, a bank loan was secured and the conversion went ahead. A large stage was constructed in the erstwhile banqueting hall of Hittle, complete with curtains and spotlights, and small antechambers became dressing rooms for the actors.

However, the seating plans occasioned the architect's greatest concern. He pointed out that the installation of ordinary seats on the existing floor would suffice, but Percy dreamed of large audiences sitting in comfort; so he insisted on curved stepwise tiers, mounting almost to the ornate though decaying plaster ceiling, bearing plush reclining seats for the hypothetical theatre-goers. The architect yielded once again. Carpenters, joiners and upholsterers moved in, costs mounted and the bank loan was extended.

At last the conversion was completed and Percy embarked on an extensive and ambitious programme, inviting top theatre companies to Hittle to stage plays ranging from Tudor to contemporary and assuring their producers that all costs would be met. His bank manager grew agitated. Perhaps all would have been well if the audiences had proved less meagre, but Hittle House was difficult to access, Percy had put only primitive parking arrangements in place, and advertising was not his forte. Expensive productions were staged before audiences smaller than the cast, and notwithstanding the ticket prices, it soon became clear that Percy would never be able to stop his overdraft escalating, let alone pay it off. The end was inevitable: the family home passed to the National Trust and Percy retired to a semi-detached house in Basingstoke.

The disaster would not have been so complete – indeed, might not have been disastrous at all – had Lord Percival not insisted on the elaborate seating arrangements. But as the architect had observed: with such plans as Percy's, Hittle Hall end in tiers.

New Beginnings

WILDEBEEST

Does the wildebeest in embryo have a *tabula rasa* within its developing brain, of the kind John Locke ascribed to humans? Locke was mistaken, and Thomas Gradgrind was mistaken, as modern-day neurobiology and developmental genetics demonstrate – not that the *tabula rasa* concept survived Kant's 'Critique of Pure Reason', save in mortally wounded form – but the idea was and remains seductive. 'The mind is a blank slate upon which experience writes': it's a simple, engaging hypothesis, which although incorrigibly wrong is still attractive, particularly when you stand at the front of the lecture theatre and behold a cohort of students, staring motionlessly past you and chewing cud. Who could doubt that the minds before you are blank, entirely blank? The blankness is writ large on their dear young faces, in their postures and body language. The most depressing aspect of the scene is that their *tabulae* will remain effectively *rasae* when you've finished teaching them. At least you get paid for it.

But there's no question that the newly-formed (or in the case of students, unformed) brain is not analogous to a newly-made digital computer, an electronic bucket waiting for software and data to be poured into it. The brain comes with its own software ready-formed, scrupulously designed to process and respond to messages from the rest of the body and, postnatally and even prenatally, from the outside world. A newly-made unprogrammed computer sits lifeless, a heap of unfunctioning electronic gadgetry. A newly-formed brain doesn't. A computer truly has a new beginning. A brain, *pace* my aspersions on the student population, doesn't. It's already begun, started from the earliest embryo stage, adumbrated in the genes constituting the recipe for its development.

But to return to the wildebeest: at least we can be sure that the wildebeest in embryo is a gnu beginning.

The Football Correspondent

Notwithstanding his passionate enthusiasm for his local team, Gordon was as objective and observant a reporter of football matches as you could meet, and the sports editor and the editor-in-chief were grateful for his services. Every week his reports on key games were lucid, balanced and informative – and occupied the right number of column inches. His personal affiliation never influenced his reporting; he was as dispassionate about the performance of his own team as of any other.

Gordon always sat in the same seat during home games. In the row in front of him sat two eccentric ladies of a certain age, who irrespective of the weather wore elaborate garments of woven silk. They were fanatical supporters of Gordon's team, and anyone who dared to belittle the team would be withered by eye and tongue. No one dared occupy either of these ladies' seats. The eccentric pair occupied the same places at every home match, as by divine right.

The Health and Safety Executive decreed that passages had to be widened; some rows had to be curtailed; some seats must be removed; and among the condemned seats were those belonging to the two ladies. Their angry representations were in vain; the row had to be shortened; the ladies were deprived of their seats. In protest, they insisted on standing at the exact positions formerly occupied by those seats. They were told that standing at matches was illegal. No one knows how far the protest would have gone had the ladies survived; but they both passed away, simultaneously. Some observers hinted that it might have been suicide.

Gordon was saddened by the demise of the two female eccentrics, though he was glad that they no longer stood at their former sites in the curtailed row because their flowing silken garb had blocked his view of the pitch. However, to his annoyance, their ghosts returned and stood in those very same positions. These apparitions were translucent, but owing to their presence, Gordon's view of the match was not as clear as he would have wished; the light had to pass through phantoms clad in woven phantom silk in order to reach his eyes.

The sports editor divined that something had impaired Gordon's vision. His reports on home games began to show a bias that had formerly been absent. He commented in detail on the shortcomings of opponents but seemed to have eyes only for the positive aspects of the home team's performances. The editor demanded an explanation for the change in style. Gordon told him about the curtailed row of seats, the protests, the demise of the two ladies and their silken-garbed return in ectoplasmic form.

'Ah!' exclaimed the sports editor. 'That explains it! You've been seeing the games through row-stinted spectre tulles!'

SLOTH

EIGHT ANIMAL SONNETS

During an evening of convivial relaxation many years ago, one of my companions raised the subject of aardvarks: *In the beginning was the Word, and the Word was 'aardvark'.* Discussion led to considerations of the odd appearance and habits of this South African anteater, and someone remarked that the aardvark could never be a subject for – say – a sonnet. To me, this sounded like a challenge.

The sonnet to the aardvark was prelude to similar essays in zoological versifying, some of which were responses to specific invitations or further challenges. One friend suggested the coatimundi, or coati, as a topic. The coati(mundi) is a burrowing rodent that lives in packs or extended family groups in the South American rain-forest. I went to see a small collection of them at Edinburgh Zoo and was struck by their morose demeanour, which could perhaps be explained by separation from their natural habitat, but served to set the direction of the poem. Another friend, returning from a holiday in Outer Mongolia, where he'd stayed for some time in a remote village called Oniu, reported seeing gerbils in the wild and invited me to write a sonnet to the gerbil, celebrating its native land.

A former colleague was amused by a set of children's crockery illustrated by an alphabetical array of animals (antelope, bear, camel, etc., through to the inevitable zebra) because no one could identify the animal beginning with 'u'. Close inspection proved it to be an unau, which is a variety of South American sloth, but I couldn't resist the challenge to write a sonnet featuring a range of animals beginning with 'u' and finally identifying the correct one. And another former colleague, who was in a difficult emotional situation because he was convinced his wife was having an affair, wanted a sonnet to remind him which of the dromedary and the Bactrian camel has two humps, and which has one. Here, we should add that not long ago, sugar could be purchased in Britain in the form of small cubes known as 'lumps'. When tea was given to a guest who took sugar, it was conventional to ask, 'One lump or two?'

I have no excuse for the other items in this collection.

In line 12 of 'Gerbil' and line 13 of 'Coatimundi' I've sacrificed grammatical correctness to the demands of rhyme. I apologise, not necessarily sincerely, to syntactic purists.

Should anyone be inclined to sing one or more of the following sonnets, here's a tune they might consider suitable:

Mark

Aardvark

AARDVARK

At midnight, when the puppies in the yard bark
And from the roof the lovelorn pussies howl,
Through Afrikaner grassland wends the aardvark
Upon its nightly ant-imbibing prowl;

And when the puppy slumbers by the spent grate,
The pussy purrs upon its fireside pelt,
Then through the darkness lumbers the oedentate
With moonlit eyes alone across the Veldt.

But when the sunrise gilds the distant mountains
And little pups and pussies all get fed,
It terminates its insectivorous outing
And burrows underground and into bed,

Saying 'Pussies and pups work hard, as I recall,
But hunting ants is the aardest vark of all.'

Armadillo

ARMADILLO

You can use an orang-utan as a pillow
Or else recline upon a kinkajou,
But you cannot thus employ an armadillo –
At least, you will regret it if you do;

For though an orang-utan's soft and pliant
And kinkajous can readily be bent,
The armadillo's outline is defiant
And as restful to relax on as cement.

Since evolution hasn't brought upon it
A dulcifying influence to bear,
An ossified and adamantine bonnet
Enwraps its little body everywhere;

But suppler mammals need think no disgrace
Of one who bravely bears so hard a case.

Camels

My Fatima, while eating bread and jam'll
Make eyes at some young drummer in the band,
Agreeing with me the while that car and tram'll
Not serve for crossing the Sahara sand;

And then when I upon my transport hairy
Seek in oasis outback tree and shade,
She lingers with that drummer in the dairy,
Doubtless discussing sonnets that I've made.

Wherefore, discussing poetry at lunchtime,
To put this poet's proboscis out of joint
She'll beg me for an enigmatic punch-line
That speaks of desert ships in counterpoint.

No more, my Fatima, we'll take our tea:
One hump for you, my love, and two for me.

Coatimundi

COATIMUNDI

A creature that eschews all joy and folly
Dwells in the darkness of the Amazon,
Its soul suffused with deepest melancholy.
I'll tell you where its *joie de vivre*'s gone.

The noble chieftain of a pack of coatis,
Whose fore-claws held the strength of ten or more,
Whose tail could lash aside a sack of tatties,
Whose snout through scent and soil alike could bore,

Who led coatimundikind to freedom,
Ate poisoned eggs one day, alas, and croaked.
They raised this epitaph – yet still they need him
And since that day they've never laughed or joked:

Res sates ponderamus et profundi;
Sic transit gloria coatimundi.

Gerbil

GERBIL

If you journey from the Khangai through Tushetu,
From Ulan Bator to the Kerulen,
Among the sand and rock and scrub I'll bet you
Will find a burrow with a gerbil in.

Wait there and watch – the rodent will not mind you.
Using another entrance that he's got
He'll creep about and come and Gobi hind you
And leave you waiting there until Urot.

From nest and storehouse of his home's interior,
Well-fed and warm and sleek, he turns Oniu
A look that is both pious and superior,
Because you don't belong there and he do.

Doubtless that is the reason why and how
He always looks Mongolia than thou.

Platypus

Odd sports of evolution's cornucopia
Remain in the Antipodes. What fuss
Nefarious jokers make, the ones who hope you'll
Insult like them the duck-billed platypus.

Taxonomists' despair, cartoonists' target,
He has done nothing to deserve such scorn.
Odd he might be, but he remains at large yet,
Ready to greet a new Australian morn.

He's just as good an animal as you are,
Yet his survival question seems to beg:
'No niche for monotremes like him, no future
Can beckon one who's furry but lays eggs'.

Useless to rail against such attitudes;
Suffice to dub them duck-billed platitudes.

U

Are you perhaps an unau of the urman
That hangs by uncate ungues underneath
Umbraceous ulmus branches to determine
How best to nibble food when you've no teeth?

Or else an urva, born of eastern races,
That forages 'mongst urio and things
And hunts for food in uliginous places?
Perhaps an urubu that's lost its wings?

Or else an urson of the northern rivers
Where ululating umiaks undulate?
Or else an urial that bleats and shivers?
Or else some yet undreamed-of ungulate?

Urially do much urson break the law
Being so unusual. Urva cheek, unau.

Unbearable Sonnet

In Leikdatz, in the middle of Bavaria,
An eastern trading man named Apun dwelt.
No swindler was craftier or warier;
He made a fortune out of selling pelts

Until, poor Apun, to a Jewish wizard
He sold a bear-skin, claiming it was mink.
This action sticking in the Yiddish gizzard
The tradesman was transmuted in a blink

Into a dancing bear, which Mordenaican
(The Jew) takes out on leash each market day,
A fate that should all rip-off merchants frighten.
Now on inquiry people point and say:

'Apun of Leikdatz? That's him over there;
Apun Leikdatz, just Mordenaican bear.'

About The Author

After he retired from a career in medicine and university teaching, Mark Henderson moved to the Peak District of Derbyshire, England, and started to write fiction and to collect and tell local folktales. In addition to a novel, an anthology of short stories and other works, he's published a collection of 62 traditional Peak District stories and tells some of them on his recently-recorded CD. He's secretary of his local creative writing group and secretary of the local concert society, and he regularly delivers talks about his work as well as storytelling gigs. He updates his website blog at random intervals.

www.markphenderson.com

About The Illustrator

David J Moss studied life drawing and portrait painting up to 1961 at Manchester Regional College of Art. On leaving college, he started work as a visualiser and was eventually promoted to creative director working on various national accounts in Manchester-based advertising agencies.

In 1965 he moved to London working in illustration studios around the Soho Square area. He also spent five years teaching at Stockport College of Technology before turning freelance as a cartoonist and illustrator. Working mostly through studio-agencies some of his more widely seen work was in book illustration. He worked on Annuals and educational children's books, including well known well known favourites from TV & Film, such as Sesame Street, Postman Pat, Mr Bean, Street Hawk and Teenage Turtles.

'Caricatures by Mossy' can be seen at the famous Sam's Victorian Chop House in Manchester. Over 200 drawings of Sam's loyal customers, are portrayed in Victorian costumes, almost covering the walls of this famous Manchester hostelry.

www.ingramcontent.com/pod-product-compliance
Lightning Source LLC
Chambersburg PA
CBHW071809020426
42331CB00025B/2813